T0145492

# The Science
# of Getting Rich
# Action Plan

**The Master Class Series**

*Awakened Mind*

*Miracle*

*The Science of Getting Rich Action Plan*

# The Science of Getting Rich Action Plan

A MASTER CLASS COURSE WITH

## Mitch Horowitz

Published 2019 by Gildan Media LLC
aka G&D Media
www.GandDmedia.com

THE SCIENCE OF GETTING RICH ACTION PLAN. Copyright © 2019 by
Mitch Horowitz. All rights reserved.

FIRST EDITION 2019

Interior design by Meghan Day Healey of Story Horse, LLC

Library of Congress Cataloging-in-Publication Data is available
upon request

ISBN: 978-1-7225-0171-6

10   9   8   7   6   5   4   3   2   1

# Contents

# Introduction

Welcome to the Master Class Series. Each of these courses teaches you, in ten simple, straightforward lessons, how to benefit from the causative powers of your mind.

The lessons are designed so that you may listen to one a day, all of them at once, or in whatever configuration you want. Do the exercises in your own time and at your own pace—but it is crucial that you *do them*. This series supplies hands-on philosophy.

This class, based on the wealth-building theories of Wallace D. Wattles, author of *The Science of Getting Rich*, augments and guides you through all you need to do to harness the author's ideas, and helps you adapt them to the special needs of contemporary life

This program is complete in itself but as a special bonus this action plan also includes a complete condensation of the original 1910 text of *The Science of Getting Rich*, which can be found in the appendix. You can use it as an introduction, a refresher, or for quick reference.

All of the programs in the Master Class Series are designed to provide you with a new estimate of yourself—and with the tools to fulfill your highest possibilities.

# Lesson
## ONE

# Do You *Want* to Be Rich?

Do you want to be rich? If you're taking this Master Class, your answer to that question may seem obvious. But look again.

In 1910, New Thought pioneer and social visionary Wallace D. Wattles published the classic guide on which this course is based. He observed then, and it holds true today, that many of us harbor deep and often unacknowledged emotional conflicts about money. These conflicts about acquiring and keeping money may go unexamined for years, or even a lifetime.

Before you begin this course, ask yourself in earnest how you *feel* about money.

If you're like me you may be surprised to discover unexplored or mixed feelings. I recall once that I was vacationing in the Central American nation of Belize, a beautiful, lush landscape of rolling hills, deep jungle forests, and winding rivers. The rustic areas of Belize are filled with legends, wildlife, and a rich and remarkable culture. We spent the first half of our vacation at an eco-lodge tucked away on a river up in the highlands. Our days were given to canoeing and walking in nature.

For the second half of our trip, we stayed at a more traditional beach resort off one of the nation's sandy barrier islands. When we arrived, I experienced a bit of culture shock: Gone were the dreadlocked guests and funky environs of the eco-resort, in exchange for the more manicured and Volvo-driving environs of the beach hotel. I could feel judgment welling up inside me about the more "establishment" nature of the beach hotel. And then it hit me: there was no price difference between the two places, but I was reacting against the "scene" of the second, as if a more obviously luxuriant setting was somehow less authentic and real. It struck me that since childhood I had harbored the unspoken notion that somehow money was compromising of one's street-level credibility or artistic or cultural integrity. I equated "being real" with a more gritty-seeming life, although the eco-lodge was, in its way, every bit as commercialized as the more standard beach resort.

I realized that this attitude was not only a needless bit of cultural conditioning, but it was—in subtle but nonetheless real ways— restraining my attentiveness and impulses toward earning money. I was, in unspoken ways, placing the earning of money on the backburner of life.

"There is nothing wrong in wanting to get rich," Wattles wrote in 1910. "The desire for riches is really the desire for a richer, fuller, and more abundant life; and that desire is praise-worthy." He is right. Money pays for education, travel, a home life, and for things like this program itself. Not everyone with money does good in the world, but generally speaking you can do greater good with money than without it. I don't know a single artist, activist, soldier, or working person who does not believe this.

Wattles understood that life stands on three pillars: "There are three motives for which we live; we live for the body, we live for the mind, we live for the soul. No one of these is better or holier than the other," he wrote.

Indeed, he noted that desire itself is potential awaiting formation; desire drives you forward: "Wherever there is unexpressed possibility, or function not performed, there is unsatisfied desire," he wrote. "Desire is possi-

bility seeking expression . . . It is in the use of
material things that a man finds full life for his
body, develops his mind, and unfolds his soul.
It is therefore of supreme importance to him
that he should be rich."

Hence, if you began this book with an
unfulfilled yearning—or even with a sense of
gnawing anxiety over your financial state—do
not be depressed or disappointed. The very
urgency that you feel is what brought you
here—and will deliver you to success.

That success may arrive slowly or suddenly,
it may be direct or indirect, it may reach you
according to your mind's-eye image or may
come in completely different and unexpected
ways. But I vow to you, as your friend on the
path, that it will come. The very needs that
drove you to this program, and to the work
of this good and foresightful man, are your
engine of progress.

Nothing is possible without some sense of
dissatisfaction with your present state—so neither fight nor fear it, but *use* it.

"Desire is a manifestation of power," Wattles wrote. "The desire to play music is the
power which can play music seeking expression and development; the desire to invent
mechanical devices is the mechanical talent
seeking expression and development."

Again, I return you to the question that opened this first lesson: *do you want to be rich?* By "rich" I mean having enough money to secure your own needs and wishes, and those of the people you love. If you can search your psyche and answer *yes*—and never turn back— you are poised on the threshold of exactly what you need.

# Lesson
# TWO

# Faith

I am not always comfortable with talk of faith. I frankly find it difficult to define, at least in a manner that speaks to everyone's experience. But it is undeniable that Wattles asks the user of his program to have faith, that is to harbor a sense of powerful inner conviction that that these ideas can and will work. He asks that you truly and really believe and accept his premises.

Specifically, Wattles wrote of three principles that require acceptance:

1. There is a thinking stuff from which all things are made, and which, in its original state, permeates, penetrates, and fills the interspaces of the universe.

2. A thought, in this Substance, produces the thing that is imaged by the thought.

3. Man can form things in his thought, and, by impressing his thought upon formless substance, can cause the thing he thinks about to be created.

He continues: "Do not ask why these things are true, nor speculate as to how they can be true; simply take them on trust. The Science of Getting Rich begins with the absolute acceptance of this faith."

So, once more: what is faith and how does one cultivate it? To some of you this question has a confident and personal answer. And I honor that. But for myself and others who struggle with faith, I offer this formula. Whenever you encounter the term "faith" substitute the word "perseverance." What is applied faith but perseverance? Work toward your aims with this in mind, determined to accept Wattles' formula while you act.

We all believe in *something*. Even the secular existentialist believes in logic and cause-and-effect. You are granted the ability to innerly select what you believe, for good or ill. So, hand in hand with perseverance, I challenge you to *elect*, for the duration of this program, to believe in Wattles' formula. After all, why wouldn't you wish to believe in something that is forwarding, affirming, and asserting of your goals? There is absolutely nothing in this program that will deter you from doing the work in front of you—quite the opposite—or that will lure you into spending ruinous sums of money, or investing yourself in distractions. This is a program that requires action and steady work. Indeed Wattles wrote:

> *You must not rely upon thought alone, paying no attention to personal action. That is the rock upon which many otherwise scientific metaphysical thinkers meet shipwreck—the failure to connect thought with personal action. We have not yet reached the stage of development, even supposing such a stage to be possible, in which man can create directly from Formless Substance without nature's processes or the work of human hands; man must not only think, but his personal action must supplement his thought.*

Possessed of this principle, you are entirely free to embrace, accept, and experiment with Wattles' core points. Let your mood be one of persistent and exuberant experimentation as you do your work. This is true and active faith.

# Lesson THREE

# Purpose

The principle of getting rich is not simply to have a good time in life. In order to attain riches, and in order to be happy once you receive them, you must have your sights set on some true, passionate, and necessary purpose.

What do you most want to accomplish in life?

It is, first and above all, vital that you have a definite and emotionally impassioned goal. Indeed, as Wattles points out, having a truly sincere and deeply held goal means that you'll have no difficulty concentrating on it, picturing it, holding it central in your mind—and thus acting on the "thinking stuff" described in lesson two. Indeed, Wattles notes: "No one needs to take exercises to concentrate his mind on a thing which he really wants."

So start there: what do you really, truly want? Be starkly honest with yourself. This is no time for embarrassment, self-limitation, or self-censorship. You don't have to announce your desire to anyone. In fact, it is better not to. Others are liable to shake your resolve. You need only share your desire with that power that resides in your innermost heart and permeates the world around us. This power is awaiting self-expression through the vehicle of your active wishes.

The purpose of life is advancement, Wattles says. Advancement is Great Creation expressing itself. "You must want real life," he wrote, "not mere pleasure of sensual gratification. Life is the performance of function."

What is your function or, put differently, your dharma? For me, one of the core purposes of life is documenting metaphysical experience, both in history and practice. I also want to be well paid for this work. I want to reach a sizable audience. I want the good things that come from money and fame. But—and I mean this with all my psyche—I will *never* make a shortcut to any of these things by neglecting truth, as I experience it. I will never offer a false or hollow idea to my audience. I will offer only those things that I know to be right and integral by way of my own search and lived experience.

I believe, and Wattles affirms, that it is vitally important, in order to attain true riches, accompanied by happiness and posterity, that your work create a circuit of productivity and offer things to people that expand their own capacities for achievement and satisfaction.

There are, of course, people who profit in negative and counter-productive ways; but I firmly believe, and Wattles supports this, that such wealth can never bring sustained happiness. The only way to earn and thrive, and to really be at home with yourself, is to fulfill a function that develops your highest sense of self, and, in some way, helps others to do the same.

Excellence is happiness.

# Lesson
# FOUR

Lesson
FOUR

# Creativity Not Competition

In the mid-1990s, I was an editor at a prominent political publishing house. I had a "friend" on staff of the kind that no one needs. He was also an editor and he sought to contact and attempt to sign up books with authors I had worked with just before I started there; he continued to do so after I arrived. His ethos was one of unbridled competition.

I responded in the wrong way by trying to match him at his own game. I failed. In two years I was fired. The firing was actually good because it put me in contact with my current work and passion for practical spirituality. The change of path helped me discover myself as a writer.

Looking back, however, if I had to do it over again and wanted to approach things in a more constructive and creative manner, I would have followed Wattles' dictum to reject the plane of competition. He wrote this in *The Science of Getting Rich:*

> *You are to become a creator, not a competitor; you are going to get what you want, but in such a way that when you get it every other man will have more than he has now . . . riches secured on the competitive plane are never satisfactory and permanent; they are yours today and another's tomorrow. Remember, if you are to become rich in a certain way, you must rise entirely out of the competitive thought.*

So, how is this actually workable on a practical scale?

Well, if I knew Wattles' work back in the 1990s I would have dedicated myself to coming up with my own original ideas, contacts, and acquisitions rather than struggling with the false perception of a limited stock of authors, topics, and book proposals.

If supply is limitless, as Wattles teaches, then we first experience this limitlessness in the mind, through ideas and thought. Ideas are a constantly renewable commodity. Conceive of your own approaches and possibilities rather than trying to corner or counter another's.

And if you cannot produce your own stream of ideas, that in itself is a valuable sign that you may be in the wrong setting or line of business. But to learn this you must first experiment: unplug from competitiveness and apply Wattles' formula. He wrote the following, with his emphasis in the original:

*Never look at the visible supply; look always at the limitless riches in Formless Substance, and KNOW that they are coming to you as fast as you can receive and use them. Nobody, by cornering the visible supply, can prevent you from getting what is yours.*

The point is that supply, like ideas, is unbounded and ever-renewing. Use this principle to escape the treadmill of anxious competition. Creativity requires no permission, and can never be taken from you.

"You do not have to covet the property of others," Wattles wrote, "or look at it with wishful eyes; no man has anything of which you cannot have the like."

# Lesson
# FIVE

# Thinking In a "Certain Way"

What does it really mean to "think in a Certain Way," as Wattles advises? In essence, Wattles is talking about adopting and holding to a mind-set of *seeing your success fulfilled*—while also working toward its fulfillment.

Follow these four steps:

**First**, Wattles prescribes getting a definite image of your aim: "See just what you want, and get a clear mental picture of it as you wish it to look when you get it."

**Second**, you must think, live, and *feel* from your vision fulfilled. Here he counsels: "That clear mental picture you must have continually in mind, as the sailor has in mind the port toward which he is sailing the ship; you must keep your face toward it all the time."

Have you ever met a person who knew exactly where he or she wanted to head in life? My sister is just such a person. As kids, we suffered through financial hardship and the fear that comes with economic insecurity. I watched as she ascended from public schools, to state colleges, to, finally, an Ivy League law degree, largely self-financed through work and loans. My sister knew precisely what she wanted, and she determinedly measured every step in life by whether it added to or detracted from her aims. She made time only for that which directed her forward on her course. That, combined with a mental image of your aim, is the force that impresses the over-mind or "thinking stuff" to collude with you in concretizing your aims. Wattles calls this the creative force of life, upon which we act through the medium of our minds.

**Third**, you must be consistent. "Spend as much of your leisure time as you can," Wattles wrote, "contemplating your picture." This is why it is so vitally important to be sure that you know what you *really* want. If you feel passion for your aim, you will have no difficulty keeping it ever before you. It won't be a burden; it will be a pleasure.

**Fourth**, you must actively work with a sense of practicality and personal progress. This is not a passive program or one of visualization alone. You are trying always to work out its "tangible expression." As I will explore in lesson seven, action is a vital complement to thought, and brings actualization to what thought envisions and coproduces.

Finally, I must cite an area in which I depart from Wattles. He wrote: "You do not need to pray repeatedly for things you want; it is not necessary to tell God about it every day." I take a different approach. Although it is true that Scripture cautions against "vain repetitions," other passages also counsel persistence in prayer. This is not contradictory. As noted earlier, faith can be seen as a kind of persistence or perseverance.

Prayer is very mysterious: It works, of that much I am sure; but the questions of when, how, and in what ways it works are enduringly and necessarily mysterious. Sometimes after reciting the same prayer again and again something just *happens*. It is not clear why or by what agency or logic. It is clear that prayer is granted to us as a kind of escape hatch from the anxieties of our psyches and the limitations of our mentalities.

Hence, I believe there is never a right or wrong way to pray. My counsel is: pray unceasingly, and pray however you wish, so long as you are sincere. Constantly picture, work, and *petition* a Greater Power for what you need. Be intelligently persistent. Change will arrive.

# Lesson
## SIX

# Gratitude

It may seem simplistic but Wattles calls gratitude the pivot point of his program. "The whole process of mental adjustment and atonement can be summed up in one word, gratitude," he wrote.

> *Gratitude opens one's sails to the winds of thought causation. It guarantees the continuation of your progress.*

Simple as it sounds, however, gratitude can be difficult to practice. The stresses of life weigh on us, and when they do gratitude is usually the first thing to go. Yet it is always possible to find things to be *truly grateful* about. This point came home to me through a comment that the actor Christopher Reeve made to NPR after he was left paralyzed from the neck down in an equestrian accident in 1995.

"I don't want to sound so noble," the actor and activist said. "There's times when I just get so jealous, I have to admit. You know, I see somebody just get up out of a chair and stretch and I go, 'No, you're not even thinking about what you're doing and how lucky you are to do that.'" Reeves comments made me realize how we overlook remarkable privileges every day. Hence, it is *always* possible to be grateful—and it is real act of obliviousness not to be.

I prescribe writing a list every morning of at least three items for which you are sincerely grateful. Look at your list from time to time over the course of your day, and read it again at night just before going to sleep. This kind of simple exercise serves as gratitude maintenance, and goes a long way toward fulfilling Wattles' principle.

# Lesson
# SEVEN

# Work Only Upon Yourself . . . but *Work*!

"By thought, the thing you want is brought to you; by action you receive it." This is one of the most important lines in *The Science of Getting Rich*. Write it down. Repeat it to yourself. Return to it. Again: "By thought, the thing you want is brought to you; by action you receive it."

People often ask about the role of personal action in mind-power programs. Some critics say—usually wrongly and usually about books they haven't read—that mind power is about passivity and idle "happy thoughts" absent personal toil and action. In Wattles' program there is no such approach and no ambiguity. He wrote with refreshing bluntness:

> *THOUGHT is the creative power, or the impel-*
> *ling force which causes the creative power to*
> *act; thinking in a Certain Way will bring riches*
> *to you, but you must not rely upon thought*
> *alone, paying no attention to personal ac-*
> *tion. That is the rock upon which many oth-*
> *erwise scientific metaphysical thinkers meet*
> *shipwreck—the failure to connect thought with*
> *personal action. We have not yet reached the*
> *stage of development, even supposing such a*
> *stage to be possible, in which man can create*
> *directly from Formless Substance without na-*
> *ture's processes or the work of human hands;*
> *man must not only think, but his personal ac-*
> *tion must supplement his thought.*

And further:

> *This is the crucial point in the science of get-*
> *ting rich; right here, where thought and per-*
> *sonal action must be combined. There are*
> *very many people who, consciously or uncon-*
> *sciously, set the creative forces in action by*
> *the strength and persistence of their desires,*
> *but who remain poor because they do not pro-*
> *vide for the reception of the thing they want*
> *when it comes.*

This also means that your wish must be *action-able*. For a wish to be authentic, rather than just fantasy or escapism, it must be connected with something that you can *do*, however small, in the here and now. A real wish is attainable, even if the means are not immediately apparent. What must be apparent is that you can train, learn, reach out to people, and labor in concrete ways that facilitate progress toward your aim.

Wattles further notes—and this is absolutely vital—that wishes come to people who more than fill their current position, job, or responsibilities. This means that whatever your present job, you must not neglect it but rather you must excel at it.

The person who *outgrows* his or her current occupation is the one who expands to the next. This is a law of life. You cannot proceed through the next phase of your existence until you have satisfied your obligations to present conditions. Greatness often appears in the person who does his or her work so well that, like a sunflower no longer fitted to a pot, the pot itself bursts and he finds himself in fresh soil beyond it.

# Lesson
# EIGHT

# Working Along Established Lines

This lesson relates closely to the one before it. The principle of working along "established lines" is one of the subtlest and most important points not only in Wattles' program, but also in all of practical spirituality. It means you must pay attention to practical channels of arrival and fulfillment. Wattles put it this way:

*In creating, the Formless seems to move according to the lines of motion it has established; the thought of an oak tree does not cause the instant formation of a full-grown tree, but does start in motion the forces which will produce the tree, along established lines of growth. Every thought of form, held in think-*

*ing Substance, causes the creation of the form, but always, or at least generally, along lines of growth and action already established. The thought of a house of a certain construction, if it were impressed upon Formless Substance, might not cause the instant formation of the house; but it would cause the turning of creative energies already working in trade and commerce into such channels as to result in the speedy building of the house. And if there were no existing channels through which the creative energy could work, then the house would be formed directly from primal substance without waiting for the slow processes of the organic and inorganic world.*

In practical terms, this means that your goal is likely to reach you along familiar or already existing channels. For example, if you seek the cure of an illness, the likelihood is not that your illness will spontaneously lift, but rather that you will discover a network of treatments that will produce your recovery. If you are looking for work, the overwhelming odds are that you will make connections and find ideas and leads that will deliver you to exactly what you need—less likely is that someone will just walk up to you and hand you, signed and sealed, exactly what you need.

Some people who practice spell work or cere-monial magick take this principle a step further. When prescribing a spell or ceremony—which is really just a ritualized intention, no different from Wattles' formula for "thinking in a Certain Way"—they note that, in order for such operations to work, there must be a clear avenue of arrival. For example, if you wish for love but dwell as a hermit there is no obvious channel of delivery. But if you wish for love and actively circulate among people, you are providing an established means or channel for your fulfillment.

Each individual must study and consider this step for him or herself. Are you asking for something that fits the context of your life, practices, and habits? Is there a foreseeable means of delivery? Or, put from a different perspective, are you neglecting or overlook-ing patterns of delivery—or perhaps the very arrival of what you want simply because it reaches you in unfamiliar ways?

I recently devised an exercise to help peo-ple work with this principle. I call it the 10-Day Miracle Challenge. It is very simple—but, as the title implies, potentially very powerful. It works according to these six steps:

1. Decide on something that you truly and passionately want in your life.

2. Write it down—your wish should be easily boiled down to a single-sentence, such as "I have a peaceful new home nearby."

3. Set a fixed period of time—in this case 10 days—by which to receive your desired element.

4. Draw a grid of 10 boxes and consecutively cross one out each day to mark your progress toward your aim.

5. Every day, often as you can and as much as you can, pray, visualize, affirm, and meditate upon the realization of your wish.

6. Finally—and here is the most important part—watch very carefully for the arrival of your aim, *and take care not to overlook or discount the means by which it arrives.*

Your wish could reach you in a wholly unexpected manner, fulfilling your need but arriving in a very different manner from what you pictured or expected. Or your wish could arrive along such seemingly mundane or ordinary lines that you are apt to miss it, and you overlook the realization of the very thing you need.

The point of this exercise is that our needs are often fulfilled, at least in potential, in ways that we are prone to neglect because the arrival doesn't resemble our preconceptions, or it happens in such a seemingly mundane fashion that we discount it.

You may, for example, wish for recovery from an injury, but at the same time reject an invitation to a movement or energy medicine class, or the sanctioned advice of a teacher, therapist, or physician, which may set you on the road to wellness Remember: *life generally works along previously established lines*. Hence, the thing that you wish for may reach you in ways that seem ordinary even though they are the royal road to your fulfillment.

I want to share a joke that drives home this point. During a terrible flood a clergyman fled to the roof of his church to avoid being swept away in the waters. A man in a raft came by and told him to come aboard. The clergyman refused. "God will save me," he said. Someone rowed by in a boat and urged him to come on it. But again the clergyman refused. "God will save me," he said. Finally, a helicopter appeared overhead and dropped a ladder. But the man waved it away. "God will save me!" he yelled. The floodwaters eventually overtook the clergyman and he drowned. Upon reaching heaven he protested to God, "I've served you all my life! Why didn't you save me?" To which God replied: "I didn't save you? I sent the raft, I sent the boat, I sent the helicopter . . ."

The lesson is: Remain open. Take the road when it appears. Reject nothing out of hand. And *never* neglect established means. Watch for them.

# Lesson
# NINE

# Power-
# Consciousness

To succeed with this program you must, as noted, select a bold but *realistic* aim; labor toward your aim; persistently and passionately hold a mental picture of your aim; persevere; and watch for the arrival of your aim through established channels. There is now one final, vital ingredient I want to highlight, and it comes not from *The Science of Getting Rich* but from another of Wattles' writings, an essay called "How to Get What You Want."

In "How to Get What You Want," Wattles talks about the importance of what he called *Power-Consciousness*. "This is what you feel," he wrote, when you know that you can do a thing, and you know HOW to do the thing."

Now, some say that positive-mind meta-physics feeds delusion. They are wrong. In fact, most people face the problem of *underestimating* what they are capable of. That is where cultivation of Power-Consciousness comes in.

Wattles prescribes a useful exercise to build your sense of Power-Consciousness:

> *Practice the following mental exercise several times a day, and especially just before going to sleep. Think quietly about the subconscious mentality, which permeates your whole body as water permeates a sponge; as you think of this mind, try to feel it; you will soon be able to become conscious of it. Hold this consciousness, and say with deep, earnest feeling: "I CAN succeed! All that is possible to anyone is possible to me. I AM successful. I do succeed, for I am full of the Power of Success."*

An important adjunct to this exercise is something mentioned earlier: to more than fulfill the responsibilities that are presently yours. Doing things greatly means doing *small things* greatly. I have found that many people avoid or short shrift the basics, which are, in themselves, a path to power and excellence. As you raise your eyes to where you wish to be take every opportunity to express your brilliance and agency by handling the things that are currently under your purview, no matter how seemingly modest.

"You can advance," Wattles wrote, "only by more than filling your present place." This is true power.

# Lesson
# TEN

# The Ethic of Getting Rich

You would experience a whole new perspective on your life if you could see how many sacrifices have been made, in a vast and surprising range of ways, in order for you to reach this present moment and experience these words.

You owe it not only to yourself but to all have suffered and labored, directly and indirectly, for your uplifting to strive toward and attain your highest station in life.

Indeed, your personal development not only pays the debts to your past and present, but invests in your future by creating a circuit of productivity that benefits others, as well. It may be argued that it is unnecessary to "get rich" in order to do all this. But having the money and resources to satisfy your desires, and those of the people you care about, is an unmistakable and productive yardstick of your success.

It is also vital, in order that your happiness be lasting and noble, that what you do to get rich be productive and up-building of the lives of others. Gossip, fakery, and con jobs can never do this. You must *contribute* to the network of productivity, which means supplying some product, service, or communication that facilitates the work of others to attain their own highest potential.

If you can check off these items on an invisible ledger, or an actual one, you need not have any hesitations or moral compunctions about doing everything you possibly can, at all times, to attain your wishes and amass personal wealth and success.

I often observe that well-roundedness is overrated. Possessing and pursuing an impassioned goal, and seeking to raise your stock and station in life, is the engine that has delivered you to this program, and that will ensure that you see through its steps. I wish you every success in doing so. The future and the present belong to those who strive and persist in self-betterment.

Go forward with every confidence in your ability. And work always to make it so.

We now turn to an abridgment of the original 1910 text of *The Science of Getting Rich*.

# Appendix

# *The Science of Getting Rich*

## Condensation

## *Chapter One*
## For Those Who Want Money

This book is a practical manual, not a treatise upon theories. It is intended for men and women whose most pressing need is money; who wish to get rich first, and philosophize afterward. It is for those who have, so far, found neither the time, the means, nor the opportunity to go deeply into the study of metaphysics, but who want results and who are willing to take the conclusions of science as a basis for action, without going into all the processes by which those conclusions were reached.

It is expected that the reader will take the fundamental statements of this book upon faith; and, taking the statements upon faith, that he will prove their truth by acting upon them without fear or hesitation.

Every man or woman who does this will certainly get rich; for the science herein is an exact science, and failure is impossible. For the benefit, however, of those who wish to investigate philosophical theories and secure a logical basis for faith, I will here cite certain authorities.

The monistic theory of the universe—the theory that One is All, and that All is One; that one Substance manifests itself as the seeming many elements of the material world—is of Hindu origin, and has been gradually winning its way into the thought of the western world for two hundred years. It is the foundation of all the Oriental philosophies, and of those of Descartes, Spinoza, Leibnitz, Schopenhauer, Hegel, and Emerson.

In writing this book I have sacrificed all other considerations to plainness and simplicity of style, so that all might understand. The plan of action laid down herein was deduced from the conclusions of philosophy; it has been thoroughly tested, and bears the supreme test of practical experiment: *it works*. If you wish to know how the conclusions were arrived at, read the writings of the authors mentioned above; and if you wish to reap the fruits of their philosophies in actual practice, read this book, and do exactly as it tells you to do.

## *Chapter Two*
# The Right to be Rich

The object of life is development; and everything that lives has an inalienable right to all the development that it is capable of attaining.

Man's right to life means his right to have the free and unrestricted use of all things necessary to his fullest mental, spiritual, and physical unfoldment; or, in other words, his right to be rich.

In this book, I do not speak of riches in a figurative way; to be really rich does not mean to be satisfied or contented with a little. No man ought to be satisfied with a little if he is capable of using and enjoying more. The purpose of Nature is the advancement and unfoldment of life; and every man should have all that can contribute to the power, elegance, beauty, and richness of life. To be content with less is sinful.

The desire for riches is really the desire for a richer, fuller, and more abundant life.

There are three motives for which we live: the body, the mind, and the soul. No one of these is better or holier than the other; all are alike desirable, and no one of the three—body, mind, or soul—can live fully if either of the others is cut short of full life and expression.

*Real* life means the complete expression of all that man can give forth through body, mind, and soul.

Wherever there is unexpressed possibility, or function not performed, there is unsatisfied desire. Desire is possibility seeking expression, or function seeking performance.

It is perfectly right that you should desire to be rich; if you are a normal man or woman you cannot help doing so. It is perfectly right that you should give your best attention to the Science of Getting Rich, for it is the noblest and most necessary of all studies. If you neglect this study, you are derelict in your duty to yourself, to God and humanity; for you can render to God and humanity no greater service than to make the most of yourself.

## *Chapter Three*
# There Is a Science of Getting Rich

There is a Science of Getting Rich, and it is an exact science, like algebra or arithmetic. There are certain laws that govern the process of acquiring riches.

The ownership of money and property comes as a result of doing things in a *certain way*; those who do things in this Certain Way, whether on purpose or accidentally, get rich; while those who do not do things in this Certain Way, no matter how hard they work or how able they are, remain poor.

The ability to do things in this certain way is not due solely to birth or talent, for many people who have great talent remain poor, while others who have little talent get rich.

Studying the people who have gotten rich, we find that they are an average lot in all respects, having no greater talents and abilities than other men. It is evident that they do not get rich because they possess talents and abilities that other men have not, but because they happen to do things in a Certain Way.

Some degree of ability to think and understand is, of course, essential; but insofar as natural ability is concerned, any man or woman who has sense enough to read and understand these words can get rich.

It is true that you will do best in a business that you like, and that is congenial to you; and if you have certain talents that are well developed, you will do best in a business that calls for those talents.

Also, you will do best in a business that is suited to your locality; an ice-cream parlor would do better in a warm climate than in Greenland, and a salmon fishery will succeed better in the Northwest than in Florida, where there are no salmon.

But, aside from these general limitations, getting rich is not dependent upon your engaging in some particular business, but upon your learning to do things in a Certain Way that causes success. It is this to which we now turn.

## *Chapter Four*
# Is Opportunity Monopolized?

It is quite true that if you are a workman in the employ of the steel trust you have very little chance of becoming the owner of the plant for which you work; but it is also true that if you will commence to act in a Certain Way, you can soon leave the employ of the steel trust for new opportunity.

At different periods the tide of opportunity sets in different directions, according to the needs of the whole, and the particular stage of social evolution that has been reached.

There is abundance of opportunity for the man who will go with the tide, instead of trying to swim against it.

The workers are not being "kept down" by their masters. As a class, they are where they are because they do not do things in a Certain Way. If the workers of America chose to do so, they could follow the example of their brothers in Belgium and other countries, and establish great department stores and co-operative industries; they could elect men of their own class to office, and pass laws favoring the development of such co-operative industries; and in a few years they could take peaceable possession of the industrial field.

The working class may become the master class whenever they will begin to do things in a Certain Way; the law of wealth is the same for them as it is for all others. This they must learn; and they will remain where they are as long as they continue to do as they do. The individual worker, however, is not held down by the ignorance or the mental slothfulness of his class; he can follow the tide of opportunity to riches.

The visible supply is practically inexhaustible; and the invisible supply really IS inexhaustible.

*Everything you see on earth is made from one original substance, out of which all things proceed.*

New forms are constantly being made, and older ones are dissolving; but all are shapes assumed by One Thing.

There is no limit to the supply of Formless Stuff, or Original Substance. The universe is made out of it; but it was not all used in making the universe. The spaces in, through, and between the forms of the visible universe are permeated and filled with the Original Substance; with the formless Stuff; with the raw material of all things. Ten thousand times as much as has been made might still be made, and even then we should not have exhausted the supply of universal raw material.

Nature is an inexhaustible storehouse of riches; the supply will never run short. Original Substance is alive with creative energy, and is constantly producing more forms. When the supply of building material is exhausted, more will be produced; when the soil is exhausted so that foodstuffs and materials for clothing will no longer grow upon it, it will be renewed or more soil will be made. When all the gold and silver has been dug from the earth, if man is still in such a stage of social development that he needs gold and silver, more will be produced from the Formless. The Formless Stuff responds to the needs of man; it will not let him be without any good thing.

The Formless Stuff is intelligent; it is stuff that thinks. It is alive, and is always impelled toward more life.

It is the natural and inherent impulse of life to seek to live more; it is the nature of intelligence to enlarge itself, and of consciousness to seek to extend its boundaries and find fuller expression. The universe of forms has been made by Formless Living Substance, throwing itself into form in order to express itself more fully.

The universe is a great Living Presence, always moving inherently toward more life and fuller functioning.

Nature is formed for the advancement of life; its impelling motive is the increase of life. For this cause, everything that can possibly minister to life is bountifully provided; there can be no lack unless God is to contradict himself and nullify his own works.

I shall demonstrate shortly that the resources of the Formless Supply are at the command of the man or woman who will act and think in a Certain Way.

## *Chapter Five*
## The First Principle in the Science of Getting Rich

Thought is the only power that can produce tangible riches from the Formless Substance. The stuff from which all things are made is a substance that thinks, and a thought of form in this substance produces the form.

Original Substance moves according to its thoughts; every form and process you see in nature is the visible expression of a thought in Original Substance. As the Formless Stuff thinks of a form, it takes that form; as it thinks of a motion, it makes that motion. That is the way all things were created. We live in a thought world, which is part of a thought universe. The thought of a moving universe extended throughout Formless Substance, and the Thinking Stuff moving according to that thought, took the form of systems of planets, and maintains that form. Thinking Substance takes the form of its thought, and moves according to the thought.

Every thought of form held in thinking Substance, causes the creation of the form but always, or at least generally, along lines of growth and action already established.

*No thought of form can be impressed upon Original Substance without causing the creation of the form.*

Man is a thinking center, and can originate thought. All the forms that man fashions with his hands must first exist in his thought; he cannot shape a thing until he has thought that thing.

Yet so far man has confined his efforts wholly to the work of his hands; he has applied manual labor to the world of forms, seeking to change or modify what already exists. He has never thought of trying to cause the creation of new forms by impressing his thoughts upon Formless Substance.

As our first step, we must lay down three fundamental propositions:

*1) There is a thinking stuff from which all things are made, and which, in its original state, permeates, penetrates, and fills the interspaces of the universe.*

*2) A thought, in this substance, produces the thing that is imaged by the thought.*

*3) Man can form things in his thought, and, by impressing his thought upon formless substance, can cause the thing he thinks about to be created.*

Read these creed statements over and over again; fix every word upon your memory, and meditate upon them until you firmly believe what they say.

There is no labor from which most people shrink as they do from that of sustained and consecutive thought; it is the hardest work in the world. This is especially true when truth is contrary to appearances. Every appearance in the visible world tends to produce a corresponding form in the mind that observes it; and this can be prevented only by holding the thought of the TRUTH.

Do not ask why these things are true, nor speculate as to how they can be true; simply take them on trust.

The science of getting rich begins with the absolute acceptance of this faith.

## *Chapter Six*
## Increasing Life

The desire for riches is simply the capacity for larger life seeking fulfillment; every desire is the effort of an unexpressed possibility to come into action. It is power seeking to manifest that causes desire. That which makes you want more money is the same as that which makes the plant grow: it is Life, seeking fuller expression.

The One Living Substance must be subject to this inherent law of all life; it is permeated with the desire to live more; that is why it is under the necessity of creating things.

It is the desire of God that you should get rich. He wants you to get rich because He can express himself better through you if you have plenty of things to use in giving Him expression. He can live more in you if you have unlimited command of the means of life.

The universe desires you to have everything you want to have.

Nature is friendly to your plans.

Everything is naturally for you.

Make up your mind that this is true.

It is essential, however that *your purpose should harmonize with the purpose that is in All.*

You must want real life, not mere pleasure of sensual gratification. Life is the performance of function; and the individual really lives only when he performs every function, physical, mental, and spiritual, of which he is capable, without excess in any.

Remember, however, that the desire of Substance is for all, and its movements must be for more life to all; it cannot be made to work for less life to any, because it is equally in all, seeking riches and life.

Intelligent Substance will make things for you, but it will not take things away from some one else and give them to you.

You are to become a creator, not a competitor; you are going to get what you want, but in such a way that when you get it every other man will have more than he has now.

I am aware that there are men who get a vast amount of money by proceeding in direct opposition to the statements above, and may add a word of explanation here. Men of the plutocratic type, who become very rich, do so sometimes purely by their extraordinary ability on the plane of competition; and sometimes they unconsciously relate themselves to Substance in its great purposes and movements for the general racial upbuilding through industrial evolution. Rockefeller, Carnegie, Morgan, et al., have been the unconscious agents of the Supreme in the necessary work of systematizing and organizing productive industry; and in the end, their work will contribute immensely toward increased life for all. Their day is nearly over; they have organized production, and *will soon be succeeded by the agents of the multitude, who will organize the machinery of distribution.*

The multi-millionaires are like the monster reptiles of the prehistoric eras; they play a necessary part in the evolutionary process, but the same Power that produced them will dispose of them. And it is well to bear in mind that they have never been really rich; a record of the private lives of most of this class will show that they have really been the most abject and wretched of the poor.

Riches secured on the competitive plane are never satisfactory and permanent; they are yours today, and another's tomorrow. Remember, if you are to become rich in a scientific and certain way, you must rise entirely out of the competitive thought.

Let us consider once more:

*There is a thinking stuff from which all things are made, and which, in its original state, permeates, penetrates, and fills the interspaces of the universe.*

*A thought, in this substance, produces the thing that is imaged by the thought.*

*Man can form things in his thought, and, by impressing his thought upon formless substance, can cause the thing he thinks about to be created.*

The supply is limitless.

## *Chapter Seven*
## How Riches Come to You

When I say that you do not have to drive sharp bargains, I do not mean that you do not have to drive any bargains at all, or that you are above the necessity for having any dealings with your fellow men. I mean that you will not need to deal with them unfairly; you do not have to get something for nothing, *but can give to every man more than you take from him.*

You cannot give every man more in cash market value than you take from him, but you can give him more in use value than the cash value of the thing you take from him. The paper, ink, and other material in this book may not be worth the money you pay for it; but if the ideas suggested by it bring you thousands of dollars, you have not been wronged by those who sold it to you; they have given you a great use value for a small cash value.

Give every man more in use value than you take from him in cash value; then you are adding to the life of the world by every business transaction.

If you have people working for you, you must take from them more in cash value than you pay them in wages; but you can so organize your business that it will be filled with the principle of advancement, and so that each employee who wishes to do so may advance a little every day.

You can make your business do for your employees what this book is doing for you. You can so conduct your business that it will be a sort of ladder, by which every employee who will take the trouble may climb to riches himself; and given the opportunity, if he will not do so it is not your fault.

## *Chapter Eight*
## Gratitude

The whole process of mental adjustment and atone ment can be summed up in one word: gratitude.

First, you believe that there is one Intelligent Substance, from which all things proceed; second, you believe that this Substance gives you everything you desire; and third, you relate yourself to it by a feeling of deep and profound gratitude.

Many people who order their lives rightly in all other ways are kept in poverty by their lack of gratitude. Having received one gift from God, they cut the wires that connect them with Him by failing to make acknowledgment.

It is easy to understand that the nearer we live to the source of wealth, the more wealth we shall receive; and it is easy also to understand that the soul that is always grateful lives in closer touch with God than the one that never looks to Him in thankful acknowledgment.

The more gratefully we fix our minds on the Supreme when good things come to us, the more good things we will receive, and the more rapidly they will come; and the reason simply is that the mental attitude of gratitude draws the mind into closer touch with the source from which the blessings come.

There is a Law of Gratitude, and it is absolutely necessary that you should observe the law, if you are to get the results you seek.

The Law of Gratitude is the natural principle that action and reaction are always equal, and in opposite directions.

The grateful outreaching of your mind in thankful praise to the Supreme *is a liberation or expenditure of force; it cannot fail to reach that to which it addressed, and the reaction is an instantaneous movement towards you.*

"Draw nigh unto God, and He will draw nigh unto you." That is a statement of psychological truth.

## *Chapter Nine*
# Thinking in a Certain Way

It is not enough that you should have a general desire for wealth "to do good." Everybody has that desire.

It is not enough that you should have a wish to travel, see things, live more, etc. Everybody has those desires, too. If you were going to relay a radio message to a friend, you would not send the letters of the alphabet in their order, and let him construct the message for himself; nor would you take words at random from the dictionary. You would send a coherent sentence; one that meant something.

When you try to impress your wants upon Substance it must be done by a coherent statement; you must know what you want, and be definite. You can never get rich, or start the creative power into action, by sending out unformed longings and vague desires.

You must have a clear mental picture continually in mind, and you must keep your face toward it all the time.

It is not necessary to take exercises in concentration, nor to set apart special times for prayer and affirmation. These things are well enough, but all you need is to know what you want, and to want it badly enough so that it will stay in your thoughts.

Spend as much of your leisure time as you can in contemplating your picture, but no one needs to take exercises to concentrate his mind on a thing that he really wants; it is the things you do not really care about that require effort to focus upon.

The more clear and definite you make your picture then, and the more you dwell upon it, bringing out all its delightful details, the stronger your desire will be; and the stronger your desire, the easier it will be to hold your mind fixed upon the picture of what you want.

Something more is necessary, however, than merely to see the picture clearly.

Behind your clear vision must be the purpose to realize it; to bring it out in tangible expression.

And behind this purpose must be an invincible and unwavering FAITH that the thing is already yours; that it is "at hand" and you have only to take possession of it.

Live in the new house, mentally, until it takes form around you physically. In the mental realm, enter at once into full enjoyment of the things you want.

"Whatsoever things ye ask for when ye pray, believe that ye receive them, and ye shall have them," said Jesus.

You do not need to pray repeatedly for things you want; it is not necessary to tell God about it every day.

"Use not vain repetitions as the heathen do," Jesus told his pupils, "for your Father knoweth that ye have need of these things before ye ask Him."

Your part is to intelligently formulate your desires for the things which make for a larger life, and to get these desires arranged into a coherent whole; and then to impress this Whole Desire upon the Formless Substance, which has the power and the will to bring you what you want.

You do not make this impression by repeating strings of words; you make it by holding the vision with unshakable PURPOSE to attain it, and with steadfast FAITH that you do attain it.

The answer to prayer is not according to your faith while you are talking, but according to your faith while you are working.

## *Chapter Ten*
## How to Use the Will

To set about getting rich in a scientific way, do not try to apply your will power to anything outside of yourself.

You have no right to, anyway.

It is wrong to apply your will to other men and women in order to get them to do what you wish done.

It is as flagrantly wrong to coerce people by mental power as it is to coerce them by physical power. If compelling people by physical force to do things for you reduces them to slavery, compelling them by mental means accomplishes the same thing.

You have no right to use your will power upon another person, even "for his own good;" for you do not know what is for his good.

To get rich, you need only to use your will power upon yourself.

When you know what to think and do, then you must use your will to compel yourself to think and do the right things. That is the legitimate use of the will in getting what you want—to use it in holding yourself to the right course. Use your will to keep yourself thinking and acting in the Certain Way.

Do not try to project your will, or your thoughts, or your mind out into space, to "act" on things or people.

Keep your mind at home; it can accomplish more there than elsewhere.

Use your mind to form a mental image of what you want, and to hold that vision with faith and purpose; and use your will to keep your mind working in the Right Way.

The more steady and continuous your faith and purpose, the more rapidly you will get rich, because you will make only POSITIVE impressions upon Substance; and you will not neutralize or offset them by negative impressions.

The picture of your desires, held with faith and purpose, is taken up by the Formless. As this impression spreads, all things are set moving toward its realization; every living thing, every inanimate thing, and the things yet uncreated, are stirred toward bringing into being that which you want. All force begins to be exerted in that direction; all things begin to move toward you. The minds of people, everywhere, are influenced toward doing the things necessary to the fulfilling of your desires; and they work for you, unconsciously.

Since belief is all-important, it behooves you to guard your thoughts; and as your beliefs will be shaped to a very great extent by the things you observe and think about, it is important that you should command your attention.

## *Chapter Eleven*
## Further Use of the Will

You cannot retain a true and clear vision of wealth if you are constantly turning your attention to opposing pictures, whether they are external or imaginary.

Do not tell of your past troubles of a financial nature; if you have had them, do not think of them at all. Do not tell of the poverty of your parents, or the hardships of your early life; to do any of these things is to mentally class yourself with the poor for the time being, and it will certainly check the movement of things in your direction.

"Let the dead bury their dead," as Jesus said.

Put poverty and all things that pertain to poverty completely behind you.

You have accepted a certain theory of the universe as being correct, and are resting all your hopes of happiness on its being correct; and what can you gain by giving heed to conflicting theories?

You can aim at nothing so great or noble, I repeat, as to become rich; and you must fix your attention upon your mental picture of riches, to the exclusion of all that may tend to dim or obscure the vision.

You must learn to see the underlying TRUTH in all things; you must see beneath all seemingly wrong conditions the Great One Life ever moving forward toward fuller expression and more complete happiness.

The very best thing you can do for the whole world is to make the most of yourself.

## *Chapter Twelve*
## Acting in the Certain Way

This is the crucial point in the Science of Getting Rich—right here, where thought and personal action must be combined. Many people, consciously or unconsciously, set the creative forces in action by the strength and persistence of their desires, yet they remain poor because they do not provide for the reception of the thing they want when it comes.

By thought, the thing you want is brought to you; by action you receive it.

Whatever your action is to be, it is evident that you must act NOW. You cannot act in the past, and it is essential to the clearness of your mental vision that you dismiss the past from your mind. You cannot act in the future, for the future is not here yet. And you cannot tell how you will want to act in any future contingency until that contingency has arrived.

Because you are not in the right business, or the right environment now, do not think that you must postpone action until you get into the right business or environment. And do not spend time in the present taking thought as to the best course in possible future emergencies; have faith in your ability to meet any emergency when it arrives.

Put your whole mind into present action.

Do not bother as to whether yesterday's work was well done or ill done; do to-day's work well.

Do not try to do tomorrow's work now; there will be plenty of time to do that when you get to it.

Do not try, by occult or mystical means, to act on people or things that are out of your reach.

Do not wait for a change of environment, before you act; get a change of environment by action.

You can so act upon the environment in which you are now, as to cause yourself to be transferred to a better environment.

Hold with faith and purpose the vision of yourself in the better environment, but act upon your present environment with all your heart, and with all your strength, and with all your mind.

You can advance only by being larger than your present place; and no man is larger than his present place who leaves undone any of the work pertaining to that place.

Doing what you want to do is life; and there is no real satisfaction in living if we are compelled to be forever doing something that we do not like to do. And it is certain that you can do what you want because the *desire* to do it is proof that you have within you the power that *can* do it.

Desire is a manifestation of power.

The desire to play music is the power that can play music seeking expression and development.

If there are past mistakes whose consequences have placed you in an undesirable business or environment, you may be obliged for some time to do that which you do not like to do; but you can make the doing of it pleasant by knowing that it is making it possible for you to come to the doing of what you want to do.

Remember always that definiteness of purpose, the ability of your thoughts to impress themselves upon the great Original Substance of the universe, the sincere impulse toward creative function, the desire to build—not to best—your neighbor, and the dedication to doing all you can wherever you are, place at your back an awesome power of Truth, to which nothing can be denied.

Build the world that you dream of for yourself and others; bring prosperity and beauty into creation; improve yourself—and you improve the world. That is the noblest goal to which any man or woman can aspire.

Thank you for taking this Master Class Course—and please explore the others in our Master Class Series. I hope this short program provided you with lessons and ideas that you will experiment with and benefit from over the course of your life.

# About the Author

**Mitch Horowitz** is the PEN Award-winning author of books including *Occult America* and *The Miracle Club*, where he writes further about the career of Wallace D. Wattles. A lecturer-in-residence at the University of Philosophical Research in Los Angeles, Mitch introduces and edits G&D Media's line of Condensed Classics and is the author of the Napoleon Hill Success Course series, including *The Miracle of a Definite Chief Aim* and *The Power of the Master Mind*. Visit him at MitchHorowitz.com.

Printed in the USA
CPSIA information can be obtained
at www.ICGtesting.com
JSHW012043140824
68134JS00033B/3233

9 781722 501716